Best Homemade Condiment Recipes

Homemade Barbeque Sauce, Mayo, Salad Dressing, Ketchup, Tartar Sauce & More

Diana Loera

Copyright 2015 All rights reserved

Without limiting the rights under the copyright reserved above, no part of this book may be reproduced, stored in or introduced into a retrieval system, or transmitted, in any form, or by any means (electronic, mechanical, photocopying, recording, or otherwise) without the prior written permission of Diana Loera and Loera Publishing LLC.

Book piracy and any other forms of unauthorized distribution or use without written permission by Diana Loera/Loera Publishing LLC will be prosecuted to the fullest extent of the law.

This page has been left intentionally blank

NOTE TO READERS

We suggest that all condiment recipes in this book be used the same day and properly refrigerated.

Some recipes state you can store the unused recipe for several days. If so, please use your discretion and common sense before using any remaining condiments.

INTRODUCTION

Have you ever realized that you forgot to pick up mayo or tartar sauce at the grocery store but didn't want to make a trip back to the store for one item?

Have you ever pulled out a bottle of Thousand Island dressing and found out it was well past the expired date?

Have you ever mumbled to yourself at the grocery store when you noticed the price of your favorite condiment has once again increased?

My wake -up call came when I saw that I was out of tartar sauce, put it on my shopping list and decided that the price the grocery store wanted was just ridiculous.

I then did a bit of research and found out how easy it was to make my own tartar sauce plus I liked the flavor much better not to mention the savings.

One of my long- time friends had given me a recipe for homemade laundry soap so I asked her if she had any recipes to make your own condiments. She did and I have included them in this book.

Some of these recipes make take more time than you have and it may be easier for you to buy the ready -made store brand. But you now know that there is another homemade option available.

Other recipes may become regular ones in your home as they save you a trip to the store and also save you money.

If you are buying the softcover version you'll see that this book is rather large. It is 8 ½ x 11 in size. I hate squinting at the font in small books especially recipe books so I don't expect you to do so either.

I've included a few color photos. I like including color photos and people who have read my other recipe books have said they like the fact that I include color photos.

The problem is, the more photos that I include the higher the publishing cost so I try to be super selective regarding photos that I include. Thank you for understanding.

Sincerely,

Diana

Table of Contents

NOTE TO READERS ... 4
INTRODUCTION ... 5
Other Books by Diana Loera ... 8
HOMEMADE KETCHUP WITH HONEY ... 9
SIMPLE AND EASY BBQ SAUCE ... 11
3 INGREDIENT TARTAR SAUCE ... 12
QUICK AND EASY COLESLAW DRESSING ... 13
1000 ISLAND DRESSING ... 14
SPICY MAPLE BBQ SAUCE ... 15
HOMEMADE GRAINY MUSTARD ... 16
HOMEMADE MUSTARD RECIPE ... 17
HOMEMADE MAYONNAISE ... 18
HOMEMADE BROWN SUGAR ... 20
HOMEMADE RANCH DRESSING ... 22
ITALIAN DRESSING ... 23
CREAMY HORSERADISH SAUCE ... 24
HOMEMADE FISH SAUCE ... 25
HOMEMADE HOLLANDAISE SAUCE ... 26
WORCESTERSHIRE SAUCE ... 27
COPYCAT A1 STEAK SAUCE ... 28

Other Books by Diana Loera

12 Extra Special Summer Dessert Fondue Recipes http://tinyurl.com/q7gpgw8

14 Extra Special Winter Holidays Fondue Recipes http://tinyurl.com/lkebggx

Awesome Thanksgiving Leftovers Revive Guide http://tinyurl.com/prxjayg

Best 100 Calorie or Less Dessert Recipes http://tinyurl.com/pn5b46c

Best Bacon Infused Dessert Recipes: 20 Mouthwatering Delicious Desserts Infused with Bacon http://tinyurl.com/owxo3pl

Coca Cola Ham, Coca Cola Cake and Other Coca Cola Recipes http://tinyurl.com/pp2wvhz

Party Time Chicken Wing Recipes http://tinyurl.com/ohsc9x8

Summertime Sangria http://tinyurl.com/oxnlnhm

Best Bacon Infused Dessert Recipes http://tinyurl.com/q38aaox

Best Copycat Recipes on the Planet http://tinyurl.com/pcuj24q

Best Pumpkin Recipe http://tinyurl.com/oxdr8fq

Best West Virginia Recipes http://tinyurl.com/oqywpbq

Best Pumpkin Drink & Dessert Recipes http://tinyurl.com/nmwx3mb

Please visit www.LoeraPublishingLLC.com to see our complete selection of books. Topics include cooking, travel, recipes, how to, non- fiction and more.

HOMEMADE KETCHUP WITH HONEY

PREP TIME: 5 minutes

COOK TIME: 20 minutes

TOTAL TIME: 25 minutes

Yield: 2-1/2 to 3 cups

INGREDIENTS:

12 oz. tomato paste

½ c. honey

1 c. vinegar

½ c. water (or more, for a thinner consistency)

2 tsp. salt

½ tsp. onion powder

¼ tsp. garlic powder

DIRECTIONS:

Combine until smooth in a saucepan.

Bring to a boil, reduce heat and simmer 15-20 minutes (you'll need to partially cover because it will spit hot tomato out at even the lowest simmer).

Keep refrigerated.

If it thickens too much in the fridge, just add some water (a couple teaspoons at a time) to reach pouring consistency.

HOMEMADE KETCHUP WITH HONEY

SIMPLE AND EASY BBQ SAUCE

Makes 4 cups

INGREDIENTS:

3 c. ketchup

2 c. brown sugar

3 Tbsp liquid smoke

1 tsp salt

DIRECTIONS:

Mix all ingredients together over low heat until thoroughly combined and heated through.

Store in the fridge.

3 INGREDIENT TARTAR SAUCE

Ingredients

1 cup light mayonnaise

1/4 cup sweet pickle relish

2 tablespoons fresh lemon juice

Preparation

Stir together all ingredients in a small bowl until blended.

Cover and chill until ready to serve.

QUICK AND EASY COLESLAW DRESSING

Ingredients:

¾ cup mayonnaise

4 tablespoons malt, cider or rice vinegar

1 tablespoon granulated sugar

1 tablespoon light brown sugar

Salt and pepper, to taste

Directions:

In a medium bowl, whisk together the mayonnaise, vinegar, sugars, salt and pepper.

Refrigerate for at least 2 hours before mixing with coleslaw so the flavors blend.

Dressing can be stored in an airtight container in the refrigerator for up to 2 days.

1000 ISLAND DRESSING

1 cup mayonnaise

1 cup ketchup

1/4 cup sweet pickle relish

2 teaspoons Worcestershire sauce

1 tablespoon sugar

Mix all ingredients until creamy and refrigerate until chilled

SPICY MAPLE BBQ SAUCE

INGREDIENTS:

½ cup coconut amino acids

5 Tbsp. of maple syrup

1 small can of tomato paste

3 Tbsp. of ground dried mustard

3 Tbsp. raw apple cider vinegar

1 tsp onion powder

1 tsp garlic powder

1 tsp sea salt

Dash of ground pepper

½ tsp cayenne (use less if you don't like it spicy)

DIRECTIONS:

Mix all of the above ingredients- except cayenne- together in a bowl until very well blended.

Add the cayenne last in little amounts for desired heat.

Brush onto meat before cooling or grilling

Store unused sauce in a glass bottle and promptly refrigerate.

Use within 5 to 7 days

HOMEMADE GRAINY MUSTARD

INGREDIENTS:

1 cup mustard seeds (use yellow, brown, or a combination)

3/4 cup apple cider vinegar

1/4 cup water

DIRECTIONS:

Place all ingredients in a covered jar and allow to sit for a couple of days so that the seeds soften.

Over the course of a couple of days, the seeds will absorb almost all of that liquid. If the liquid is completely absorbed and your seeds look a little dry, add a bit more water. (The absorption rate varies by seeds.

After a couple of days pour the contents of the jar into your blender and process until the mustard is the desired consistency.

Less if you like it grainy, more if you prefer it creamy.

Pour the finished mustard into a clean glass jar that has a lid and promptly refrigerate.

HOMEMADE MUSTARD RECIPE

INGREDIENTS:

1/4 cup of brown mustard seeds

1/4 cup of yellow mustard seeds

2 cloves of garlic

1/3 cup of filtered water

2 tablespoons of organic apple cider vinegar

1 teaspoon of salt

2 tablespoons of whey

Juice of a small lemon

DIRECTIONS:

Let the seeds soak overnight and then drained them. Soaking seeds, nuts and grains before cooking allows for the production of numerous beneficial enzymes which contain many vitamins. The soaking process also breaks down difficult to digest proteins into simpler components which are easier for the body to absorb.

Add all the ingredients into the food processor or blender and blend. Pour the mixture into a bottle, and cover with paper towel or cheesecloth and a rubber band. Let it sit on your counter for 3 days. You will begin to see bubbles in the mixture and will see a yellowish liquid at the bottom of the mixture within 24 hours.
 After the 3rd day you can remove the paper towel/cheesecloth and mix the mustard. Pour into a clean glass jar with a lid and promptly refrigerate.

HOMEMADE MAYONNAISE

Makes 1 cup of mayo

INGREDIENTS:

1 whole egg

1/2 tsp dry mustard

1/2 tsp salt

2 Tbsp. white distilled vinegar

1/4 cup vegetable oil

1 dash paprika (optional)

3/4 cup vegetable oil

DIRECTIONS:

In a blender, add all ingredients except the last 3/4 cup oil.

Blend on low for 2 minutes.

Then, with blender still running, take the cap off the lid, insert a funnel to reduce splattering, and slowly pour the remaining 3/4 cup oil into the blender as a thin stream. (Pouring too quickly will cause the mayo to be runny.)

Continue blending for a few more seconds, or until thickened; it doesn't take long.

Promptly put your mayo in a glass container with a lid and store in the refrigerator.

HOMEMADE MAYONNAISE

HOMEMADE BROWN SUGAR

1 cup granulated sugar

1-2 tablespoons molasses (depending on how dark you want it)

In a medium bowl, add molasses to sugar and mix with a fork or using a stand mixer fitted with a whisk attachment, working up to high speed, until no big clumps of molasses remain. This'll take several minutes.

You may need to use a fork to break up clumps and there may be some tiny clumps remaining when you are done but the end result will be worth it.

Store in an airtight container.

Homemade Brown Sugar

HOMEMADE RANCH DRESSING

INGREDIENTS:

¾ cup mayonnaise

¾ cup sour cream

1 tablespoon lemon juice

1 small bunch of fresh chives

1 small bunch of fresh parsley

1 clove garlic

1 tablespoon olive oil

½ teaspoon paprika

½ teaspoon salt

¼ teaspoon pepper

¼ - ½ cup milk (depending on desired thickness)

DIRECTIONS:

In a food processor or blender, blend all ingredients.

Allow flavors to combine in the refrigerator before serving.

ITALIAN DRESSING

INGREDIENTS:

1 cup vegetable oil

1/3 cup red wine vinegar

1 tsp salt

1 tsp sugar

1/4 tsp dried oregano

1 tsp yellow mustard

1/4 tsp paprika

1/4 tsp dried minced garlic

DIRECTIONS:

Mix all ingredients in a glass container with a lid.

Shake well.

Refrigerate for at least 2 hours before using for the best flavor.

Shake well again before serving.

CREAMY HORSERADISH SAUCE

INGREDIENTS:

1 cup sour cream

1/4 cup grated fresh horseradish

1 tablespoon Dijon mustard

1 teaspoon white wine vinegar

1/2 teaspoon kosher salt

1/4 teaspoon freshly ground black pepper

DIRECTIONS:

Place all of the ingredients into a medium mixing bowl and whisk until the mixture is smooth and creamy.

Place in the refrigerator for at least 4 hours or overnight to allow flavors to blend.

Sauce can be stored in the refrigerator in an airtight container for up to 2 to 3 weeks.

HOMEMADE FISH SAUCE

INGREDIENTS:

2 cloves garlic, coarsely chopped

Zest from 1 small lemon (optional)

3 tablespoons finely ground sea salt

6 bay leaves

2-3 teaspoons whole black peppercorns

1 1/2 pounds small whole fish (smelt, herring, etc)

1-2 cups non-chlorinated water, as needed

2 tablespoons sauerkraut brine or fresh whey or 1 teaspoon additional sea salt

INSTRUCTIONS:

Muddle the garlic and the lemon zest together with the sea salt.

Rinse the fish, then cut them into 1/2-inch pieces. (If they're too big, you'll end up with lovely pickled fish, but not much sauce.)

Toss the fish pieces (including the heads and tails) in the muddled salt mixture to completely coat the fish. Add in the peppercorns and bay leaves, then lightly pack the mixture into a clean 1-quart mason jar, pressing down on the pieces as you go to release the juices.

Pour the sauerkraut brine or whey into the jar, then pour in as much water as needed to completely submerge the fish, but be sure to leave at least 1-inch of headspace at the top of the jar, as the mixture will expand as it ferments.

Cover tightly and leave at room temperature for 2-3 days, then move to the refrigerator and let sit for 4-6 weeks.

Double strain the mixture through a fine sieve or cheesecloth and discard the solids. Store in glass bottles in the refrigerator for 4-6 months.

HOMEMADE HOLLANDAISE SAUCE

INGREDIENTS:

3 egg yolks

Pinch of pepper

1-2 tbsp. fresh lemon juice

1/2 cup salted grass-fed butter

DIRECTIONS:

Prepare immediately before serving, it only takes a few minutes to make and you will want to serve it fresh

Place eggs yolks, pepper, and lemon juice in your high-powered blender

Heat butter over a medium-high burner until it is hot and foamy

Put cover on blender and blend yolks until beaten, only a few seconds

Then, with the blender on med-high speed, slowly pour in the hot butter — very slowly so it emulsifies

Watch out for splatter out the top of the blender- it will be very hot so use care.

Continue until butter is all gone, your mixture should be thick and creamy.

WORCESTERSHIRE SAUCE

Makes about 1 cup of sauce

INGREDIENTS:

1/2 cup apple cider vinegar

1/8 cup molasses

1/8 cup soy sauce

2 tbsp. honey

1 tbsp. fish sauce

1 tsp pepper

1 clove garlic

1 tsp onion powder

1/2 tsp chili powder

1/4 tsp cinnamon or ground clove

1/2 tsp ground ginger

Juice from 1/2 lime

DIRECTIONS:

In a small saucepan, mix ingredients together and bring to a boil. Reduce heat and simmer for 10 minutes.

Remove from heat and pour into a blender.

Blend until smooth.

Store in a dressing bottle, or covered bowl in the refrigerator for up to 1 month.

COPYCAT A1 STEAK SAUCE

INGREDIENTS:

½ cup water

½ cup balsamic vinegar

¼ cup Worcestershire sauce

¼ cup ketchup

¼ cup. Dijon mustard

¼ cup seedless (golden) raisins

½ teaspoon celery seed

½ teaspoon kosher salt

¼ teaspoon black pepper

½ tablespoon chili sauce

2 cloves garlic, minced

⅛ large yellow onion, sliced

1 large orange

DIRECTIONS:

Add all ingredients (except the orange) to a small pot. Cut orange in half and squeeze each into the mixture and then place them in the pot. Bring to a boil, stirring constantly. Reduce heat and simmer for 10 minutes.

Grab a bowl and a mesh strainer and pour the mixture into the strainer (you don't want the big pieces – you want a smooth liquid).

Allow to cool and pour into a clean A-1 bottle or air-tight container.

Store in fridge.

www.ingramcontent.com/pod-product-compliance
Lightning Source LLC
Chambersburg PA
CBHW041231040426
42444CB00002B/124